Colette Bryce grew up in Derry and currently lives
in the north of England. She has published four previous
collections with Picador including *The Whole & Rain-domed
Universe* (2014), recipient of a Christopher Ewart-Biggs Award
in memory of Seamus Heaney. *Selected Poems* (2017) was
a PBS Special Commendation and winner of the
Pigott Prize for Irish poetry.

T0347057

Colette Bryce

The M Pages

PICADOR POETRY

First published 2020 by Picador
an imprint of Pan Macmillan
The Smithson, 6 Briset Street, London EC1M 5NR
Associated companies throughout the world
www.panmacmillan.com

ISBN 978-1-5290-3750-0

1 3 5 7 9 8 6 4 2

A CIP catalogue record for this book is available from the British Library.

Printed and bound by CPI Group (UK) Ltd, Croydon, CR0 4YY

Visit **www.picador.com** to read more about all our books
and to buy them. You will also find features, author interviews and
news of any author events, and you can sign up for e-newsletters
so that you're always first to hear about our new releases.

Contents

The M Pages

Death of an Actress

She has, as chimney sweepers, come to dust.
And bitten it. She has given up the ghost
and lies in cold obstruction there to rot
where angelstubs perfect untimely frost,
now she. Frights me thus living flesh
does yield soft saply to the axe's edge.

Has gasped her last, pegged out, gone west.
Mislaid the future like a set of specs
or a loop of keys. Has booted the bucket,
dimmed her light to the glownub of a wick
and snuffed it, passed unto the kingdom of perpetual
night, hooked up with darkness as a bride.

Shuffled, mortal. Crossed the Styx into
history. She has joined the great majority,
sloughed off her body like a costume coat
discarded on the carpet. *Dearly departed*
sleep, bed down with beauty slain
and beauty dead. Black chaos comes again.

A London Leaving

Out of breath I spot
the polished lozenge of a hearse
pull beside me,
beetle-backed,
nose towards a church.

I quicken foot, I fall in step,
frightened, but of what?
The fear of god is not
the fear of god but fear
of fungi, rot.

Open-arsed it then
from which the surgeons
ease a planky box.
Six, before the entry arch.
Danny Boy, How great thou art.

A husband's silver stubble.
Baritone at the earhole.
A fiddle-thumbed
accordionist from Brecht,
into your hands, O Lord . . .

Grave politeness,
blot appearing underarm
at seams of shirts.
A poem fished from Google search,
Do not stand for it, she's dead.

We, instead. Tapered heels
of ladies
sinking into earth.
Athenry: a man recalls
a drubbing at a rugby match.

'Sorry . . . trouble.' Loosened knots.
Uisce beatha,
two fingers, stop.
Smokers in the parking lot,
ashes to ashes,

'yes, we must
in happier . . .' Some awkward hugs.
Glitter webs on the railings.
Travel apps and Uber cabs.
Splash dispersal on a map.

Cuba

1

Each classic carapace cruising on the Malecón

each buffed up candy-coated shell
with back seat sizzling for half a century
like a steak
appears beyond a veil
a shimmer screen of heat on asphalt.

Each billboard grievance propa-propaganda

Each teetering theatrical colonial façade
would fold like a losing hand of cards
they said
       (think Buster Keaton, squared
in a window frame)
       and yet   it didn't.

2

An aperture
      in the throat of a beggar
hole   bole in the bark of a tree
in which a tocororo might hole up or huddle
in which a guerrilla might stash a cache.

Reach in if you dare with tweezer fingers
draw out a voice
a slim streamer of words
      like the ribbon of an ancient typewriter
      held to the light
on which is embossed
in mirror type   that bold assertion
      regarding history's absolution.

3

Standing in line at the breadline pharmacy
standing in line for half a century
the next cashier will see you shortly
                rest assured.
'La ultima?' Sweat is tickling
sweat is trickling down your spine.

If only a pen   you would write this down.
If only a Bic or a Biro refill
        Our Man in Havana
        The Writings of Fidel
if only a party pin for your lapel
a beard and a cap
            and a manual of manoeuvres.

4

A twenty-two foot Che at Santa Clara
in silhouette
        we are wilting at his boot.
Is that a rifle or is he pleased to see us?
The triumph of fist and gun over
        fist and gun.
Such monoliths now recall Saddam
alas   mid-fall   (you quash that thought)
a world at tilt and the law of entropy.

Under armed guard
        this monumental Che
ensures the military sensibility
prevails   alongside Christ-face ubiquity.

5

Two cockatiels are trilling from a cage
in piercing voices
          (greasepaint cheeks
complete the impression of a Punch & Judy),
are swinging topsy-turvy from the perch.
'It's hard but not impossible to get a visa out.'

On a box television circa 1984
(the tube quite bust
          its vintage distortions
take you back   in time the retinas adjust)
a Brazilian soap might strike the right note
but the bathroom sort
          remains elusive.

6

Rum, rumba! Rumbo in the jungo
is a killer cocktail
      (we mustn't grumbo).
Rumdumb   meaning drunkard or drunk
is a pleasant condition
      and you think *Ron Collins*
sounds like someone you really might have known

back home.   Miguel Alfonzo Francisco
Wilfredo   skinny old-timers in the Plaza
soft shoe salsa for a couple of cucs
and the rattle of maracas or begging cup
(guaranteed *bona fide*
      Buena Vista Social Club).

Perfect Smile

The time has arrived again to attend
to my bite, now that my bark is perfected.
Time to attend to my toothstones, chisels,
choppers, nippers, laughing gear,
my string of pearls, my wolfish incisors,
molars, mashers, porcelain shelves,
'a newer Sèvres pleases, old ones crack'.

*

Three teeth, he says, holding up three fingers.
Jaws sink down into warm putty; the soft
fwap of removal, muttered approvals,
Paris attacks on the news, before
some asinine pop that takes you back.

'Okay?' Fine. The shrill malarial
whine of the drilling enters your brain on
burning threads as your grip on the armrests
tightens, jaws widen, ache
like the jaws of a python measuring up
to the unexpected breakfast of a goat.

*

Eyes shut, you retreat to a tropical island
far away, perhaps that very one
where Selkirk was *kinggovernmentandnation*.
The snake will require a longish siesta
after this, while you retrieve your coat

from the hook on the door and slink
through reception with its ad campaign
for *Invisalign*, 'the clear alternative
to braces', into the aircon cavern of your car
to inspect each fang in the rear-view mirror.

Needles to Say

The stitched mouth
of censorship.

The numb lip and cheek
of anaesthetic,

slurrish diction
Ishhouldliketomakeaspeesh.

Needles to say,
painful to articulate.

Drum

There's a broken pane in the window of my ear,
the act of a vandal: a black triangle.
The pigeons are in and it will take a renovation
to reclaim. Alas, there are no plans pending
and a grey dove peers out early most mornings
through the murk, surveying the street below,
harried commuters slanting to their work.
Where the pigeon retreats to, I don't know,
but often the window holds only unfathomable
dark, and the flag of a black triangle.

It may be, in fact, a succession of pigeons
playing the bird at various points
of its life; like the hair wash scene by Almodóvar,
where a woman bows down over a basin
then emerges from the towel a different
actress than before – older, sadder, lined –
like an early photographer rising from the cloak
of her machine to a world devoid of colour.

A Final Day on Earth

A shrunken sack of bones
a swirl of fur
he sleeps beneath the sum
of all his years
while flies detect the scent
of death and sketch
a spirograph of interest
round his skull
delicate
as the eardrum of a whale
you held once
in a peninsular museum.
From time to time
he flicks his old striped tail
a half-spent reflex
failing to deter them.
One crisp ear
forested with crosshairs
manages a twitch
defunct divining dish
while sunken darkened orbs
(now flecked) would seem
lately to have blown
their frazzled filaments.

Lifted – gently
underneath the oxters
he concertinas down
to twice his length
a slinky spring
paws prissily *en pointe*
and unimpressed
at this last inconvenience
the long zone
of his underbelly feathery
soft as fledglings
cradled in his mouth
when *Jaws* that
two-note theme was once
his erstwhile soundtrack
round the verges.
So long tomcat
thanks for all the mice
we'll miss you
though you were grumpy
always pernickety
to the bitter end
old foe old friend
old tightarse Moriarty.

My Criterion

She writes *New Englandly*.

How do I?

Derrily? Verily.

Irelandly? 'Northernly.'

Emigrantly, evidently.

The White Horse

after Adomnán

When the saint's old bones wouldn't journey
any further, he paused for a breather,
sat down by a verge
that was humming with the unfinished business of spring
and there, the old workhorse approached him.

The animal nuzzled its long white skull
to Columba's chest
and wept, softly,
tears from its pale-fringed eye blotting
the shirt of its master, weary by the roadside.

Diarmait, embarrassed, tugged it by the rope
instructing the animal back to its duty,
but the saint shook his head
and mouthed 'Let it be'
allowing the white horse to pour out its grief,

stroking the salt-soaked bristles of its muzzle,
the two of them kindred
in the knowledge of his death.
Blossom in the hawthorn, tiny lights;
a halo of flies around both of their heads.

Hire Car

Later, my iPhone delivers up the name –
Fend Flitzer – this snub-nosed rental calls to mind:
Invalid carrier and direct precursor
of the Messerschmitt, which famously vroomed
on billboards by Saatchi in the late nineties,
around the time you finally quit,
quietly, against all expectations:
too late, Mammy, your lungs already shot.
For decades that was your brand, *Silk Cut*.
What was that advert's message all about?

I can vaguely remember a spike or fin,
as we ease you from the wheelchair, bend
your hinges into the hatchback (memory foam
on the seat for your sore, score brittle bones),
fasten the belt across you with a click.
Not forgetting your tank, 'Jacques Cousteau':
the soundtrack in your house is the slow *whiissht-coo*
of the oxygen in the downstairs bedroom's
constancy, its breathing for you.
These days, the smallest excursion is a win.

Unreachable inside a room / the traffic parts
to let go by, we'll go for a spin as far as Grianan,
stop in at Doherty's on the way back
for a sugared cappuccino and a Derry bap.
Nozzles in your nostrils, tubes about the ears,
hearing aid: we untangle your glasses.
Handbag, blue badge, paracetamol . . .
His hands on the oar / were black with obols.
Are we right? All set? I remember now
what it was about that car: no reverse gear.

Fungi

In the time-lapse
footage of the
decomposition
of a pear,
a light lace crust
appears
and devours
the fruit
which collapses
in on itself
like a beast
brought down
by a pack.

Always, fungi
is feasting,
working
its quick
saprotrophic
magic on all
matter, even
this seasonal
litter I've just
finished clearing
from your grave,
your shelf
of the earth,
                    yes you,

who don't
even realise
you're dead.

The M Pages

Golden lads and girls all must,
As chimney-sweepers, come to dust.

Shakespeare, *Cymbeline*

There's nothing doing here, you know that, don't you?

first response paramedic, July 2017

i.m. MB, with love

1.

M has disappeared and that's final.
That's final: the ultimate words
in a reprimand when we were small.
'You are not going out, and that's final',
calling an end to the argument.

All I wanted was for M to be okay:
a circle of family, friends, the drop-in
centre, the basics to sustain. To be,
if not happy, then *happy enough*.

Day 1. *Nothing doing*. I wish
there'd been a warning, a scare, a chance
to show more love, to change
the course of events.

But 'No', scolds the universe,
'It doesn't work like that. Final
is final.   And that's   that.'

2.

The great nothing breached like a whale
and submerged again, just to remind us,
or rather inform us it is always there,
all times, all place,
monstrous in the depths.
M is no longer.
M is no longer.
No not never non M.

*

'She'll be back in no time', we used to say
to indicate an imminent return, but now
it is literal, fit to apply
to our pre-human position, condition, and hence,
post-life, to be back in no time once
again, alone, and eventually nameless.

*

When all of those who know to attach
the word for your person, picture or voice,
to you, are consigned
to no time, too,

your name will unfix like a limpet from its scar
and birl away
in the ocean's eddies,
a waltzing teacup, and you, dear M,
plus all of us, will become unspoken.

*

I'm nobody, who are you?
As nobodies, we do not do.
A greeting from the other side, the ether side:
Are you nobody too?
Are you not, like me? I could use some company.
The dead 'forgets her own locality'.
Have you forgotten us, M?
Do you know the way home?

*

Dying is an art you were not very good at.
You brought the element of surprise,
at least, a bumbling unpreparedness.
Caught in the act, one could say, messy.
A take-me-as-you-find-me
sort of style.

You shucked off your body like a winter's coat,
discarded on the carpet.
Dearly departed.

When I found you, M, you had already gone
like vapour from a stone,
the window open.

3.

Someone is clutching
the master key.

'In these circumstances',
she speaks quietly, 'the police
would normally go in first.
Are you certain you want
to enter as next of kin?'

I failed to notice then, but already
the terminology of death.

She slots the key in the lock,
I cross the threshold
into the dim-lit hall. *M,
are you there, M?* Knowing
not knowing. Part of me

expecting to find her passed
out on drink, or over-doped
on the medication,

something *retrievable*

calling for comforting words,

like *Come on Sis,
it's not the end of the world.*

4.

An outsize sergeant in the narrow hall
in bullet-proof vest, Northern Ireland style,
looks like he might be around eighteen,
a bobby on the beat from Camberwick Green.
'Obliged to attend at an unexplained death',
he explains, in a tiptoe duteous voice.
Would I be so good as to identify
the body to him, so that he can confirm in turn
to the state pathologist in Belfast,
etcetera? Yes, I understand.
He tilts towards me, clipboard in hand:
'Can you confirm that is Colette in there?'
'*M*, you mean?' You couldn't make it up.
He looks for a moment blank, then twigs:
'Oh my goodness me, I'm terribly sorry.
Please confirm it is your *sister's* body.'

5.

The *Whatnot* shop on Market Street
where you would acquire little overpriced items
that snagged the eye:
silvery knick-knacks,
curios, trinkets
attractive to a child.
They must have seen you coming,
we used to sigh: credulous you,
with more money than sense.

Elsewhere, I'd get incensed
at wily traders, taking advantage.
The Canon digital camera, for example,
when you didn't even possess a computer
to process the shots.
The miraculous medal
at £50. For that piece of tat?
It all amounts to little,
after the fact. The fact being?

Death. Nobody wants
our accumulated stuff.
What is meaningful? What is not?
What not, M?
How's it going out there?
Or (cliché) here, in my heart
(groan). Only, you're not.
What are you, so, if not you? What now?
Wherefore did you go?

6.

M on the slab, in the undertaker's lab
in ghastly make-up, beige foundation.

M in the procrustean bed of the coffin,
M one of *them*, the dead.

M in the glass display case of the hearse,
a legend in daisies, S-I-S-T-E-R.

M on her own, up front, at the altar,
M the unwitting subject of the lecture,

walked down the aisle by six tearful sisters –
M as a bride, M having died –

and her only brother; awkwardly lowered
on ropes down into a six foot crater

filled by a neat municipal digger.

We stall in silence
                              gradually disperse

like images on the surface of a stream

            into which a stone is cast.

7. The Whereabouts of M

Don't let's talk about the underworld and all that crap.

I open the door to the flat
in the silence after, trying to locate
some essence of M amongst the clutter,

but I can't find her –
not in the novels bundled
every which way on the shelves,
various pages bookmarked for return.

A fine fair hair floats out and glimmers in the air.

Nor is she in the pocket volumes,
Thought for Today, *The Courage to Change*,
in the trinkets, beads, the strewn CDs,
the tiny totally-out-of-control kitchen –
bin bags spewing open on the floor,
dishes abandoned on every surface –
a *nature morte*, arrested overwhelm.

Unopened packages from Bradley's Pharmacy,
unfilled prescriptions, scattered blister packs.
Bottles of Chardonnay, full, and empty,
oil paint tubes, dishevelled costumed dolls.

Accumulations of coins in stashes,
euros, pounds – the border currencies –
kilos of metal sinking bags and bowls.

Cupboards crammed with unwashed clothing,
coats, shoes (she'd acquire more, new).
The practically inaccessible bathroom.
Our Lady of Sorrows gazing from the wall.

A rain stick's hoard of seeds
lies silent in its husk, pays heed
to the law of gravity.   I recall
her body, the blood having clustered to the front,
livor mortis, where she'd fallen
forward by the bed. Red-purple. *Lividity*.

A glass-bead mobile shivers at a draught
from the door; I move to take my leave.

The whereabouts of M, I'm afraid,
are simply unknown.

She must have gone out someplace.

She has not come home.

8.

A phrase on the radio: *avoiding the overwhelm*.
A month's mind. *Nothing doing here.*
What happens to the selfhood after death?
A naïve question. Is there even an 'after'?

Is death an illusion? Is 'life' extinguished?
Or does it go on, the soul and all of that?
Hey, where exactly does a *person* go?
Hello? Look here, we could use some answers.

Hilary Mantel once wrote of seeing ghosts,
of portals through to a post-death zone.
Beyond Black: a motorway medium
flanked by a cynical sidekick, Colette.

The mind fills up with Victorian charlatans
cashing in on the vulnerable bereaved:
mechanical doorbells hooked up to a wire.
A ouija board. *Knock knock. Who's there?*

Yet . . . I'd love to imagine some semblance
of joy, in some other realm, for M.
A self-serving thought. Her own thoughts,
brief in a notebook, branded 'Paper Blanks':

It isn't as if
I have anyone to answer to
I live on my own

I am not beaten yet

I am paying respect to my past
which over the last
three years has been
drink drink drink

I will hang on
to this sobriety for dear life

It is very much living in the day

9.

I hope you were drunk when you died, M,
if that could mean you would have suffered less.

In the inward zone; comfortably numb.
A distant ship's smoke on the horizon.

Body slumped with the random clothes
on the cluttered floor of your tiny bedroom,

M you had flown, skedaddled, cleared

right out. I thought to cover the mirror,
windows were open (things I read in books),

but I knew full well that you had done a flit,
had given life the slip, your route quite clear.

No one here. Only the body,
the leftover cumbersome difficult body.

10.

M's face is kind of loose, provisional.
Caked in make-up, we used to say
in our teens, meaning over-applied Max Factor.
Dontlooktooclosely. 'If you look here,
closely, under the chin, you can see
that the skin is starting to loosen',
says the dreadful undertaker, tugging
at the neckline's rucked satin.

He is recommending a closed coffin
for the wake. 'Even by tomorrow, worse'.
Jesuschristjesus. A small perforation
in the skin near her jaw, where the elasticity
has snapped. The size of a little fingernail.
We all notice. Like the zombie dramas,
all the rage these days on screen.
He takes his leave. Her sisters and brother

gather in. M's face looks swollen,
pasty, set in mock repose, and still
recognizably hers, but also wrong.
We stand around her, awkward, vaguely
alarmed. Why haven't they shown her hands
as they normally do, interlaced with a rosary?
Her fingertips looked blackened at the scene.
Has the skin begun to corrupt there also?

Dontsayanyofthis. Closed coffin.
'Tomorrow the condition will be worse'.
We think she must have died on the Friday,
meaning . . . *Christ*, she lay three nights. *One*
cannot bear so much reality. D calls up
M's favourite song online, Sandy Denny,
Who knows where the time goes, rests
the phone on her shroud. We all join hands.

11.

Your hands persuaded her into shape,
the sculpted form of a woman sitting,
straight-backed, relaxed, legs tucked under.
A dreamer, sure; her stillness palpable.
Next, a fine-tooled texturing of skin,

cross-hatching of cloth, a patient finish:
your own image, lately come to rest
on my studio sill, the garden abundant
in the glass, the final flush of summer,
one year on, and nothing to be done.

I love the tranquillity of the pose,
interior gaze, a self-containment
close to that you always had in life.
Upstairs, in a walnut jewellery box,
is your charm bracelet, carefully unclasped

from your wrist in the mortuary in Belfast
they'd brought you to, all on your own,
and sealed in a plastic bag with your ring
and watch that kept on marking time
long after time had ceased to matter.

The clay retains a mortar chill. I weigh
it in my hands. It is all too much,
your absence, turning it over, writing this,
adding lines to sorrow's lines that only
serve to assert that you are gone for good,

to cast in words the unbelievable fact.

12. *A Digital Photograph of Your Grave*

Your first birthday after your death.
A bed of snow and you tucked in.
Its cellular composition
widens on my phone, then shrinks:
a winter's scene. Your social
media account that perseveres
in time, somewhere, has announced
this marker of a year
to brightly exhort your circle
to wish you happy. I wish
you had been happy. Halfway

around the world I can feel
the marrow chill of that cold soil
where you are actual. Lately
we talk about monuments
on the family blog; we say, absurdly,
that you would have liked
a bird in flight, or a Celtic knot . . .

But for now, a simple cross
stands watchful at the plot, a host
to hothouse blooms –
incongruous in the circumstance
as everything, as birthday cards.

13.

I like your grave. The place, I mean.
Odd times, I feel an expansive gladness.
A new allotment in the old cemetery,
at the foot of the hill, light and skyful,
overlooking the football grounds
and the Brandywell's dramatic grotto:
the Virgin in her hollow, Medbh in her grave.
I've only noticed the rhyme, you'd have liked it,
smiled at that, which is a presumption
to say, as lately we do, so often:
'she'd have liked this, would have loved that.'
What you like and what you'd choose
to shine your childlike love upon
is moot, forever, never to be known.

14.

Forever, never to be known.
I draw a line beneath the line
and puzzle it. To never wake,

never stagger to your feet
and sway, unsteady in the small bedroom
(Sorry, it's all been a terrible mistake).

To never breathe a word of it.
To never speak no more, a split
infinitive; no not never in a month

of Sundays (Monday, it was, I found you),
not, as they say, in a million years,
at no point ever, not, non.

Say it: dead. *In perpetuity.*
Continually, incessantly, repeatedly dead.
Say it: gone . . . The language

strains – *for ever and ay,*
for ever and a day – and ultimately
fails: *for a very long time.*

Apartment

The quietness in rooms suspends
like throngs of weightless polystyrene balls,
closely but not densely packed,

so that, advancing,
you enter an electric caress
as it parts and closes around you.

How would you breathe?
A flaw in the dream? Perhaps
you could don a snorkel mask – and only this –

as you swim through the silk molecular bliss
of your living room, exulting
in the morning.

21 Westland Row

Blue, the morning. Green, the lights.
Raucous the calls of Liffey gulls,
soft and dolorous the bells.

Low, the doorframe. Silver the pushbutton
lock with its code C-X-2-8,
its basement entry, awkward opening.

Steep, the stairs, many the flights.
Hot the cardboard coffee cup.
Urban, the view of slated roofs

and redbrick pointing; café, pharmacy,
foreshortened passengers
rushing from the Dart.

Yellow, a fleck in your paisley shirt
you scrutinize in a daydream . . .
Concentrate.

Yes: famous the birth.
Famous the Oscar Wilde
who was born.

Here is the room where Oscar Wilde.
He fought the law and the
law won.

Here is the actual spot.
Short, the leap to Merrion Square.
Happy the formative years

Slander

after Anna Akhmatova

Slander accompanied me everywhere,
its stealthy footfalls creaking in my dreams,
and the muted finger-patter of its keys
as I walked the streets of a numbed city
searching for consonance and warmth.
Its pin-point light appeared in every eye:
shame, suspicion; often worse.
I was not afraid. I held on to my words
and answered each fresh accusation.
Lately, I see the inevitable day
my friends arrive, with tinted windscreens,
pulling up at kerbstones in the dawn,
stooping over my sleep and sobbing,
lacing a rosary through my hands.
Then, surreptitiously, slander will enter
the room, and sit, where my blood chills,
her pursed and fretful mouth rehearsing
a grievance-list of imagined offences,
quietly at first, notes intermingling
with rhythmical prayers for the dead.
Soon they repeat her delirious lies
and no one dares to meet another's eyes,
when out from my body, frozen in the void,
freed at last of its mortal frailty,
my soul steps up to its bold occasion,
rising into the dawn's blue mist
to blaze, once, with fierce compassion
for everything I have lost.

The Family Reunion Show

At last he will meet the lost parent:
she who marshalled off her brood
and left him in a hostile place
to fend for himself with the rough
children, far from sight and mind.
He'd like to reject the rejecting parent
but he longs for her, longs
to be noticed and loved. But his
is a futile yearning. The woman,
who made her Sophie's choice,
now hates more than anything else
to be reminded. So the man rehearses:
'It's okay, Mother, it doesn't matter.
It doesn't matter that the people to whom
you gave power over me despised me
and starved me. Look, I'm still alive.'
Today is the day. He arrives early,
takes his seat on the set
        and straightens his tie.

An Amendment

Dublin, 2015

A
family tree
with its fine-wire hangers
in tiers   is a piece
of the history of the universe
a trinket mobile
suspended from a shelf
a flimsy wind chime
of births   marriages   deaths
and offspring   ad infinitum
An ever-   animate affair
it shivers   in response
to a breath
the slightest   disruption
in the air

A Short Commute

Ushered onto the bus by their mother,
two little girls. One with a blonde Labrador
in high-vis vest with the legend AUTISM, the other
in her wake, as the woman bleeps a permit
on the scanner, steering dog and smaller child
who at once erupts in a crimson rage,
rejecting the seat selected by her mother.

The older girl, in glasses like her mother,
sits on a little drop-down seat
facing us all. She is dressed in a cream fur coat
like the pelt of a baby seal, so velvety plush
and so pristine it could be fresh from the shop.
Anxious, finely attuned to a slight
kerfuffle round her furious sister,

she offers placating words along the aisle,
her face a study in worry, compassion,
disappointment and, yes, loneliness,
the various moods rippling across
in response to a sensitive family radar.
She begins to sing to herself, a traditional song
in a high wavering voice, *Báidín Fheilimí*,

and I notice other passengers
glance up at her, but she sings it quietly, barely
audibly, gazing out at a slideshow of buildings
flashing past in colours on the glass,
sometimes swerving her gaze to locate
the mother and sister, tranquil now
with lowered eyes, counting on fingers.

I want to acknowledge this pensive little girl,
to say 'Hey, that's a beautiful coat'
or some such thing to make her smile,
but already I reach my stop and step
through the exit doors and the bus pulls off,
its speed increased beyond my pace, and a thread
is snapped and the moment passes.

A Last Post

My ideal job?
Inspector of the tideline,
the ocean's eyebrow,

after the sea
has sucked in its breath
and closed its lashes. I'd live

in a wrecked Bishopean shack,
the lion's paw prints massive
in the sand, and always

in weather like this,
in tattered old shorts
and a vest, my skin salted.

A currency of driftwood
and feathers, necklaces of wrack
like cured leather,

I'd collect in a basket
to barter with the wind.
With shells and fish hooks,

alphabet of bird bone
and twig, I'd fashion
flotsam poems, in my utter

element, pottering along
far from the roar
and heat of politics.

Odd times, a hound
might spring out of nowhere
after a ball, an anoraked owner

in its wake; or I'd wave
to the lone kayaker, buoyant
always as a bath-toy in the waves,

but really, at home
with my own company
I'd be; barely curious enough

to track those trails
of human spoor to the point
at which they always disappear.

NOTES AND ACKNOWLEDGEMENTS

Death of an Actress – 'chimney sweeper', via Shakespeare, is a Warwickshire dialect term for the dandelion seed-head.

Cuba – 'History Will Absolve Me' is the title of a four-hour speech made by Fidel Castro in 1953. The typewriter on which it was written remains in the Museum of the Revolution, Havana.

My Criterion – the Emily Dickinson reference is to her lyric 'The Robin's my Criterion for Tune –'

Hire Car – 'Unreachable inside a room . . .' from 'Ambulances' by Philip Larkin; 'His hand on the oar . . .' from 'Charon' by Louis MacNeice

The M Pages – 2. 'I'm nobody, who are you?' Emily Dickinson; 'forgets her own locality' ibid.; 'Dying is an art', and 'you do not do' Sylvia Plath

9. 'A distant ship's smoke on the horizon' Pink Floyd, 'Comfortably Numb'

Acknowledgements are due to the editors of publications in which some of these poems first appeared: *Bath Magazine*; *Causeway to Causeway*; *Female Lines: New writing by women from Northern Ireland*; *Icarus*; *The Irish Times*; *Poetry International*; *Poetry Ireland Review*; *Poetry London*; *The Poetry Review*; *The Tangerine*. Thanks to first readers Bev Robinson, Linda France and Martha Kapos, and to my editor Don Paterson.